How to Stop Procrastination

Learn How to Manage Your Time Wisely and Stay Productive

Ambreen Hameed

Contents

Introduction

Procrastination is the art of putting away a task, undertaking or objective for a later time. It is prioritizing catching up with some episodes of your favorite TV Series overwriting a report that is due for submission. This means that you are procrastinating on the more important task.

That said, taking a deep look into the meaning of procrastination, you will find that it basically has to do with postponing a more important undertaking for something which is less essential, but ostensibly more alluring. With the example of writing a report, you find watching your favorite TV Series more fun than writing a report due for submission, so you find yourself invested more in the former even though you are aware of the importance of writing the report.

Occasional procrastination is not quite harmful. To be honest, all of us have been guilty of procrastination at a point and may have put away specific tasks even regularly. In as much as occasional procrastination does not negatively affect our lives or hamper our abilities to achieve our set targets then it's okay.

Procrastination becomes dangerous when we engage in the act for too long and develop the habit of putting things away when we have something essential to do.

Even the most organized people are not immune to procrastination. They sometimes spend considerable hours on less important things like surfing the internet aimlessly or binge-watching their favorite sitcom when they know they ought to have spent those precious hours doing something more important.

Plainly speaking, occasional procrastination may not be harmful, if you become lost in the act of constant procrastination, then it can have an adverse effect on your productivity and by extension your happiness and prosperity.

Ways Procrastination can Compromise Your Life and Well-being

- Reduces Your Productivity: Among the first and significant effect of procrastination is that it limits your productivity. Ordinarily, when you keep setting aside your tasks until the last minute, you keep heaping up the task, and the moment you eventually begin to work on the task, you have so much work before you that you end up abandoning the work instead of seeing it through. This keeps you from attaining your set objectives and getting closer to the many dreams you have in life.

- Affects Your Discipline: When you continually delay doing something you should do, you soon develop the habit of procrastination. Constantly giving in to distractions reduces the inner resistance that helps you to resist temptations. Soon your ability to exert self-control weakens and before you know it, you completely lose the self-control you once possessed to do what is correct and important. To maintain self-control weakens and before you realize it, you completely lose the discipline you once had to do what is right and essential.

- Shakes Your Self-Confidence: Continuous procrastination will eventually start to affect your ability to deliver at your work. It will affect your ability to work efficiently and deliver at a level expected of you because you have gradually lost the ability to work hard and believe in yourself. This dwindles your self-confidence, and you stop performing at the level you should.

- Increases Your Stress Levels: Stress can be easily associated with the inability to deliver as you should or not fulfilling your objectives. Ordinarily, when you begin to fall short of targets or failing to beat a deadline, have multiple tasks to fulfill, feel a drop in confident and unable to resist distractions, your stress levels increases which also adds to your challenges.

- Affects the Quality of Your Life: If you are controlled by your attraction and not by your own determination, you will continue to submit to unnecessary distractions. Instead of doing what is correct and important you will continue to work on frivolous tasks and never achieve the sense of fulfillment and satisfaction you require to feel happy. Procrastination can also get in the way of your routine activities, personal development, and responsibilities towards yourself and those around you. All of this affects the quality of your life and hampers your chances of having a fulfilled life.

In simple words, procrastination can come in the way of you having a purposeful life. It can get in the way of your plans and aspirations which can lead to frustration. To gain self-confidence, develop discipline, become strong and have grit so you can gather better control of your life procrastination is one dangerous habit you need to break. Let us now move on to the next chapter and discover the first step you need to take to get closer to this objective.

Chapter 1:
Don't Be a Perfectionist

This may quite appear like the complete opposite of the previous chapter, but irrespective of the determination to overcome having impulse control, any attempt at being perfect is complimented by slipping or making mistakes.

One of the important tenets that accompany emotional intelligence that we discussed earlier is not only the power to avoid making sudden decisions as it relates to avoiding emotions, but also the ability to maintain balance. People who possess emotional intelligence can detect when their emotions or thinking is irrational and not contributing to their overall well-being. So, when they face difficulty to fulfill a goal or task and they find themselves having negative thoughts like "I should have done better" or " I'm never going to beat this deadline" they are able to discover the negative effect these kinds of mindset have on their mood and mental state. A person who has a grasp of their own internal emotions will be able to self-correct to prevent from falling into a series of the negative mindset and into a downward spiral.

Having a constant ongoing environment of negative mindset about yourself does not encourage anyone to work efficiently on those tasks or objectively and instead only serves to pull that person into a pit of negative opinions about their abilities, and destroy their motivations to complete tasks. I know that the idea of beating yourself into submission may appear like it makes sense at first glance.

You may think that somehow a constant reminder that you cannot afford to fail, and cannot dare to "screw up" should gear you towards noticing mistakes and avoiding them. Instead, it creates an atmosphere of self-doubt, fear, and sadness. Anyone who lives in an environment of doubt isn't likely to be capable of overcoming other negative emotions and will sooner give into impulses and distractions, because now they are experiencing the negative environment of lack of confidence and anxiety alongside the uncomfortable feelings of stress over working on a task or the need to create time out to study with friends. Adding more overwhelming negative emotions to the mix does not make things easier, and is a form of sabotage.

Being easy on yourself and simply noticing where you can make changes, from a natural angle, is more positive and keeps you on task much longer. Accomplishing great feat doesn't usually follow a simple straight line. Mistakes are also learning opportunities instead of failures. Learning from every mistake and making new commitments to change provides an opportunity to grow your self-discipline.

Chapter 2:
Build The Intention To Break Procrastination

Every journey to a achieve an objective begins with a commitment; a commitment to improve, to develop better control of your impulses and to work with dedication and perseverance towards the objective to eventually actualize it.

A lack of strong commitment and a clear intention to achieve a set objective, you are quite likely not going to move dedicatedly towards it. This is why it is important that your journey towards breaking procrastination begins with an unwavering commitment as well.

Make a Strong Commitment Backed by Compelling Whys

Now that you have identified your challenges and committed yourself to fix it, you need to reinforce your commitment and strengthen it by pin it in a compelling way. You need to have a convincing reason or even several reasons why you need to overcome the dangerous habit of procrastination, so you can apply dedication towards your goal.

The whys associated with every goal drives you to work towards achieving the goal because they are the reasons why you are chasing that goal. If there is no compelling reason why you wish to break procrastination, then why would you ever attempt to? If losing weight isn't important to you, why would you ever go to the gym and focus on a diet? To overcome procrastination, you need to discover the reason why you wish to do it.

Close your eyes or even keep them open if you want and consider your current shortcomings. It could be your struggle with losing weight or the challenges you are experiencing in starting up your business or how you are facing depression and the urge to give in to it or anything else that is significantly adding stress to your life and restraining you from living how you truly wish to live.

Put down your findings, and if you evaluate your work routine and compare the amount of time you spend on actually important tasks and those you wasted on meaningless things, you will realize that procrastination is a significant reason why you are finding it difficult to achieve your desired goals. Consider how your life would change for the better if you build up the courage to resist your temptations and overcome procrastination to do the important task. Write down those reasons and let them motivate you in your quest to overcome procrastination.

Set a Clear Goal

Determine the reason you need to defeat your urge to procrastinate and why you are more motivated than before to work towards this very goal, set a precise goal to actually beat this dangerous habit. You can have several goals on your list that you would like to fulfill in other to have a more meaningful and happy life, but it quite daunting to work on several goals at the same time.

Understand that your willpower to work on a certain task reduces with every move you make towards a certain goal.

Therefore, if you work for 3 hours straight on analyzing customer feedback for your Company's product, you are likely to feel drained after that and might not be able to carry out another high priority task for another couple of hours.❌

To ensure you don't run out of willpower to work on anything significant at all, take it slow and steady. It is good to make a list of the objectives you would like to work on to become active, excited and productive, but select one important one from the list that you would like to start with.

See that you make the goal as clear and precise as possible, so you know exactly what you are trying to achieve. If your goal is to improve your grades, make a plan for the type of grades you will like to have and compare it to your current grades and determine the areas you will need to work harder. If you procrastinate on starting a hobby think about how you want to go about it and create a specific goal based on it. Once you have better clarity on your goal, write it down.

With the list, you now have compelling reasons to overcome procrastination. Next, you need to draw up a set of an action plan to work positively towards this goal and confront every temptation that comes your way. The next chapter shows you exactly how to do that.

Accept Your Problem

To develop a clear intention to overcome your problem, you first need to admit that there is a problem to address in the first place. Unless you acknowledge your problem, you will not come to appreciate its full effect in your life and you will not be able to work diligently to solve it.

Coming to terms with your problem becomes easier when you concentrate on how it is affecting your life. To do that, do the following:

- Evaluate your daily activities starting from the time you wake up time to your bedtime and write down all tasks that make up your routine. Do write down the amount of time you devote to every task.

- Now consider the essence of every task on the list and think about the benefit you derive from each task. For instance, if you spent 2 hours researching the internet for information about a particular subject, what results did you achieve after that research? Were you able to carry out meaningful research or were you not entirely pleased with your findings primarily because you did not devote 3 full hours to researching on the topic? Think about whether or not every task you do daily helps you achieve anything meaningful in the end.

- Consider how much time you invest in the tasks on the list and how much of that time is spent on other activities. If you spent 2 hours drafting a pitch to a potential investor in your business, think about what you actually did in those 2 hours. Did you spend those two hours thinking about the content of the pitch and research on it to ensure that you created a convincing pitch or did you spend half of that time using social media and spent only half doing the actual task?

- Moreover, try to consider the task you plan out daily, but somehow end up not doing. Write down those tasks and compare their essence and determine the result each of them would have helped you to achieve with the tasks already put on the list. If you had intended to write an article for a blog, submit a proposal to some firms, visit an old school friend in the other part of town, do some household chores and preparing dinner, but you ended up only writing the article and doing laundry, why do you think that happened? What went wrong and where did it go wrong that altered your plans for the entire day and made you fall short of achieving your set targets for the day?

Once you have comprehensively written out all the answers to the questions and have evaluated your routine, go through your activities a couple of times and from your evaluation, you will realize how often you are culpable of procrastination and how harmful it is for you. When you compare the results you achieve every day with the objectives you hope to achieve, you will instantly come to the realization of how your habit to postpone important tasks and engage in something less meaningful but obviously more entertaining while putting off working on an important task is actually a bad habit that is only harming your life. This realization will help you to come to term with your challenges.

It is important to make a verbal backed with a written declaration of this acceptance to openly face your challenges. Say and write down, "I have a bad habit of delaying important tasks, and I am going to work hard to overcome this habit steadfastly." Your declaration can be in different words but the message should be the same.

Chapter 3: Exploring Habits and Their Impact on Self-Control

Habits play a significant role in the type of person you are and in your level of output. To effectively improve your self-discipline, you will require a strong understanding of habit making that the ones that have become part of you. This chapter takes a deep into habits and supplies comprehensive information about habits so that you are able to make the positive changes you require.

What Are Habits?

By definition, a habit is a regular or settled practice, behavior or tendency. They are anything we find routine, and over time becomes natural. You likely carry out many habits without even really noticing it. For example, for most people, it is a habit to get out of bed in the morning, use the restroom and grab a quick beverage. This becomes routine, and every time you wake up, you do those actions in that order without even really thinking about it.

Habits can be positive or negative. For example, smoking is an example of a bad habit. Bad habits tend to have a strong grip on you and can become easily addictive and difficult to break. This is because there are countless other additional behaviors associated with them, and each behavior needs to change order to overcome the bad habit. Procrastination and overspending are two other common habits that are very addictive and have no positive impact on your life but are hard to break.

Positive habits can have a great impact on your life.

Why are habits so vital to your level of self-discipline? You have numerous habits that you unconsciously carry out every day, but maybe you don't feel disciplined yet. Your level of productivity and discipline are directly impacted by the habits you keep. If you have several bad habits, they are likely going to negatively impact your productivity and happiness. For example, if you are a smoker, think about how many times per day you take time out to engage in the habit. It likely adds up to an hour or more of not doing anything productive. If you were to get rid of this bad habit, you could have an extra hour to devote to doing something more positive. If you regularly lose track of time and are chronically late, you lose the trust and respect of other people over time; how much more closely would you get to achieving goals if people in your life help you out because they knew they could count on you? Instead, a bad habit robs you of both valuable time and trust.

Now, when your good habits outweigh the bad ones, this allows you to effectively manage your life. Good habits give you the mindset to focus on a higher level of what is important to you. When people tend to have more good habits, they can reason better and think clearer in general, and tasks that might appear complex becomes naturally easier to think about and to tackle.

Your habits have influences over other aspects of your life. It is much easier to develop what we call "bad habits" because they often provide a sense of immediate pleasure and satisfaction. For example, a person might smoke a cigarette or stress eat because to provide them with calmness and satisfaction at that moment. However, over time, these moments of pleasure can create big problems in your life. Smoking can have terrible health consequences, and stress eating can have a grave impact on your physique and your personal life. This also plays into gratification, which is discussed in a subsequent chapter.

Habit Development

In December 2012, a paper published in the British Journal of General Practice looked at habits and the psychology behind them. One study analyzed in this paper evaluated habit development and what it takes to make a behavior automatic. The participants chose a behavior that was healthy, such as taking a walk or eating a piece of fruit. They also chose a cue, such as doing the activity directly after breakfast. After approximately 66 days, the frequency of their chosen behavior started to slow. They missed the occasional routine, but overall, this did not slow the ultimate progress of the habit. After missing it once, the automaticity of the habit could still be resumed.

This study displayed that when you are working to develop positive habits, it will not be easy to forget about them once the foundation is set. The key is putting in the effort to develop the habit of a state of routine.

In August of 2014, the Society for Personality and Social Psychology studied people's daily lives and how habits play a part in our activities. They estimate that approximately 40 percent of the activities that you do each day is routine. They attribute this to associative learning. The research shows that once you discover behavior that brings you closer to accomplish your goals, you seek to repeat these patterns. Associations start to form between response and cues as a result.

The process of habit formation starts within the brain's basal ganglia. This is said to trigger a three-step process, which is the habit loop you will learn more about next. Over time, as the habit-loop continues to be performed, the brain essentially gets involved less and less, making the process of performing the habit one of routine and once the associated cue occurs.

Habit Loop

The habit loop is a type of neurological phenomenon that governs any specific habit that you might have. There are three elements associated with it, including a routine, a cue and a reward.

The cue element is really anything that causes a habit. Common categories for these cues include:

- Location
- People
- Preceding action
- Time of day
- Emotional State

For example, if you normally get a coffee at 2:00 pm, once 2:00 pm hits, this is your brain's cue to go and get a cup of coffee. Perhaps you always get an ice cream treat at a certain restaurant, and now every time you go to that restaurant, you crave the treat. The cue can be strong and can feel almost like an obligation. Cues can become varying levels of positive or negative for your life, depending on the habits that they are associated with.

The routine is the behavior of your habit. For example, you physically going to retrieve the coffee at 2:00 pm would be the routine in this example or buying the treat you crave at that restaurant.

The reward is the reason that your mind remembers the habit, and why it is worth remembering. For example, that coffee makes you feel relaxed or gives you a boost of energy to get through the remainder of your workday, or the treat tastes like a delicious reward at the end of your meal.

This loop is what can also make bad habits so difficult to break. First, you have to recognize your cues. Then, you have to alter your behavior. Lastly, you have to recognize that the reward that you are getting is not as great as it seems. Now, when you are working to build positive habits, you want to use this loop to ensure that they become strong enough to overpower the bad ones essentially.

Chapter 4:
Effective Ways to Fight Procrastination

Inability to Make Decisions

Indecision is the arch nemesis of our ability to take action. Think of indecision as the Joker to your Batman of taking action. That basically describes everything you need to know about it. It paralyzes us and makes it impossible to move forward, rendering us ineffective and useless. Until we break out of this loop of deliberation that ultimately leads to indecision, we cannot move forward.

When we come to these cognitive forks in the road, we contemplate the options in front of us before moving forward. This is a natural and beneficial process. It helps us to select the options that best compliment our goals and circumstances.

But some folks get caught in a deliberation loop. They get stuck at the contemplation stage. They continue to go over the possibilities and permutations of the events, eventually, they end up doing nothing.

In the absence of a sufficiently-compelling incentive to act – for example, a boss threatening termination – the delay becomes perpetual, losing control of their choices and sadly costing them a lot.

Indecisiveness can stem from many factors, some of which we've already explored.

For example, an individual may be worried that choosing an inferior option will cause him or her to be unsuccessful (fear of failure). He may be concerned that choosing poorly will force him to produce imperfect work (perfectionism). She might fear that making the wrong selection will generate unappealing results (aversion to risk). A person might be uninterested in the options before them and the absence of a challenging option leads to not choosing any (boredom). For somewhere to begin a particular task is what constitute their bone of contention and series of deliberation (uncertainty of where to begin).

I speak from personal experience. I used to have trouble choosing between multiple options, leading to procrastination on my part or in some cases, inaction. Here are a couple of simple tactics I used to overcome this problem.

How to Overcome Laziness

First, identify the reasons you tend to be lazy. Some people are lazy because they harbor a low self-image. Others are so because they have absolutely no interest in the task at hand. Still, others use laziness as a coping mechanism when they're faced with a task they find disagreeable.

Although laziness is considered by many to be a natural character trait, there's usually a root cause that triggers the behavior. The key, as always, is to identify that trigger.

Second, identify obstacles you believe are preventing you from taking action. Ask yourself whether these obstacles are truly impossible to overcome. When you scrutinize them, you may find they're little more than mirages. They either don't exist, or they're far less impactful than you imagine. They may even be invented as a way to rationalize behavior.

For example, suppose you're trying to motivate yourself to go for a jog. A possible "obstacle" might be that you don't know where you left your running shoes. But this isn't likely to be a true obstacle. After all, there are only so many places your running shoes could be located in your home. In this example, the "obstacle" has been invented to rationalize laziness.

Third, get into the habit of taking action. Most people who struggle with laziness believe the issue stems from a lack of motivation. In truth, motivation is fleeting for everyone. What separates the action taker from the excuse maker is the habit of acting.

The good news is that this habit, like all habits, can be learned. The key ingredients are time and consistent application.

How to Overcome a Low Tolerance for Adverse Events

I used to have this type of mindset. Small problems bothered me a great deal, often to the point that I couldn't focus on anything else. It was an irrational way of thinking, and almost always led to my putting things off.

Here's a brief rundown of them:

First, I came to realize that my intolerance for distress was mostly in my mind. That is, my agitation when things didn't go my way wasn't due to external stimuli. It was due to the way I internalized those stimuli.

For example, having to wait 30 minutes for a table at my favorite restaurant wasn't causing my distress. My impatience was causing it.

Second, I developed the habit of grading each adverse event on a scale ranging from one to 10. One meant an event was harmless. Ten meant it was worthy of DEFCON 1. By grading events, I was able to put each one in perspective.

For example, hitting a red traffic light, while inconvenient, was far less severe than having my car totaled in a traffic accident. As such, it warranted a far lesser reaction. Rating the red traffic light accordingly gave me a more practical outlook.

These measures gradually made me more tolerant of circumstances that got in the way of immediate gratification. As a result, I became less inclined to put things off and better able to handle the frustration of things going differently than planned.

To be clear, I wouldn't describe myself as a stoic. But I'm no longer fearful of the distress and discomfort posed by adverse events.

If you struggle with low frustration tolerance, I encourage you to try the three steps I've described above. You may find they radically change the way you perceive everything that happens around you.

How to Overcome an Inability to Make Decisions

Taking action short-circuits our impulse to procrastinate as we wait for additional details to make better decisions. This is good because we rarely need more details. In most cases, we simply convince ourselves that we do in order to postpone making a choice between competing options. It's our way of dealing with fear and discomfort about the unknown.

The important thing to remember is that this fear and discomfort are rarely warranted. The true cost of choosing a less-than-ideal option is usually negligible. Meanwhile, the cost of allowing fear and discomfort to rob us of our ability to make decisions is significant; it sabotages our productivity.

In addition to making a commitment to take action in the face of uncertainty, it's important to grow comfortable with making imperfect decisions.

This is a practice I used to great effect in conquering my own indecisiveness. I developed the habit of asking myself, "What's the worst that can happen if I choose the wrong option?" In most cases, the effects of the worst case scenario wasn't that devastating. In fact, the result was just simply less positive than choosing the ideal option.

For example, I would agonize over choosing a restaurant to host a get-together with friends. Should we meet at a Mexican restaurant? Or do I pick a Chinese restaurant? Maybe a gourmet burger joint would do? These and many more questions like these I ask myself resulting in me overthinking the whole situation – and in the process, I become paralyzed. Naturally, I'd procrastinate the decision, often to the point that it became impossible to make a reservation.

Ultimately, the choice didn't matter. The worst-case scenario was that we'd endure poor service or imperfect food. But that was a risk with all of the restaurants. The truth of the matter is that we at the risk, regardless of the venue.

Here's the takeaway: if you struggle with indecisiveness, get into the habit of taking action. Stop overthinking and deliberating over your options – make a decision and you'd find out that the results may not be as different from the options you have forgone.

How To Overcome An Aversion To Hard Work

The most effective strategy I've found for taking action on difficult tasks is to have a system in place. This has to do with having a preset schedule and to-do lists that gradually become habits over time. With a system in place, you don't need so much motivation and willpower before carrying out any activity or taking an action – all you have to do is follow your schedule.

If you regularly procrastinate because you're averse to hard work, I strongly recommend that you try the following approach. Suppose you'd like to create a side business to generate extra income. Building any type of business is hard work.

If you think of creating a side business in those dismal terms, you'll face a lot of internal resistance. You may put off tasks integral to building the business, and instead focus on things that promise to be more fun and immediately gratifying.

Having a system in place helps you deal with internal resistance - for example, you might commit to working on your side business from 6:00 p.m. to 8:00 p.m. daily. When you repeat this over a period of time, it becomes part and parcel of you and gradually it becomes a habit you cannot do away with. Even without any motivation, you will still get your work done.

Another thing you can do is to identify any three tasks that are pivotal to catapulting your business into a thriving one and commit to getting them done every morning, immediately after waking up from sleep. When there is a system in place, your worry would cease to be about time and effort – instead, you begin to focus on results. And more importantly, you're developing the habit of taking action on a daily basis.

Assuming you're addressing the right tasks, your daily effort should ultimately produce your desired results - in our example, a business that generates a side income.

How to Overcome Boredom

Boredom as a result of a task can stem from a number of reasons – one, your heart may not be into the task (this is just like my personal example above), sometimes the boredom might come as a result of repeating a task several times. Many people get bored after carrying out a task for a long time. Another reason you can get bored by a task is if the task is not so important.

Your approach in overcoming the boredom will depend on the reason for such boredom.

If your heart's not into a task, try to change a few things about the task in a way that your mind is stimulated towards it. Get creative with the task in such a way that you would need multiple skills or the involvement of people whose skill are required and the company you would enjoy.

If you're working on a repetitive task, create a little game that makes performing it fun. For example, how many envelopes can you stuff in 20 minutes without making a single mistake? If your coworkers are doing the same task, make a fun and friendly game out of it.

If you're not sure why the task at hand is important, ask a superior for clarification. If you don't have a superior - for example, say you're a freelancer, stay-at-home parent, or a college student - determine whether the task needs to be addressed at all.

Boredom is self-imposed. We control the triggers that make us feel bored. That means we can develop tailored strategies to help us conquer our boredom, and thereby overcome our need to procrastinate.

How to Overcome Uncertainty About How (Or Where) To Start

If you're feeling paralyzed by a mountain of work, the best thing you can do is simply start. Pick a task and address it, ignoring everything else on your plate.

It doesn't matter which task you pick. You'll find out eventually that you'll gain momentum once you get started. This momentum would carry you into the second one, and then the next one, and so on till you complete the task at hand.

If you're procrastinating because you don't know the best course of action to take on a project, reevaluate the potential outcomes associated with different approaches. There's a good chance you're envisioning a potential catastrophe when the likely outcome of a particular approach is far less serious.

This type of procrastination comes from a fear of failure. We fear the worst, even if the outcome is improbable at best. This fear paralyzes us and prompts our brains to seek distractions in the form of more relaxing and comforting options like watching a movie. Hence, you end up procrastinating.

If you lack the information necessary to complete a task or project, figure out the simplest way to obtain it. Then go ahead to pursue that option even if it poses several challenges. For example, if obtaining the information requires you to seek help from someone you dislike, especially if the person's help is essential to the completion of the task – grin and bear it, as a matter of fact, make use of the opportunity to extend an olive branch to the person.

That's good news because it means we're ultimately in control. Taking action banishes doubts, and replaces them with self-confidence. It also prevents the brain from seeking distractions as a way to avoid the distress borne of uncertainty.

How to Overcome A Feeling Of Overwhelm

There are a few questions that you need to ask yourself. First on the list is – why are you feeling this way? Then, ask yourself what exactly is causing you to feel overwhelmed? Only then can you create a plan for tackling the triggers and resolving the feelings that are holding you back.

For example, suppose you're feeling overwhelmed because you're not getting enough sleep. Your nerves are frayed, you're irritable, and minor annoyances are magnified. In this case, insufficient sleep is a trigger. You'd need to come up with a plan for getting the sleep your mind needs to perform effectively. Get to the root of the causes of insomnia and rid yourself of those worries.

Suppose you're feeling stressed because you're juggling multiple projects. The fragmented focus is the trigger. Here, it's helpful to break down each project into its constituent tasks. Then, address each task one by one.

Suppose you're feeling overwhelmed because a loved one has died. In this case, therapy is the advisable remedy.

How to Overcome Fear of Success

The challenging part about conquering this fear is that you can easily miss it. We would often mistake fear of success as a meek procrastination instead of considering it as a cause of our procrastination.

First, look for signs that make you delay taking action because you're fearful of success. Ask yourself whether getting appreciation concerns you. Are you bothered that others might see you as a fake? Are you worried that you may not carry out as expected?

Second, ask yourself what might come about if you do well. Seemingly, you find that your greatest fears are baseless. Remember, fear, in all of its manifestations, is powerful because it hides from view. When we confront it head-on, it becomes powerless.

Third, ask yourself whether the outcome of success is consistent with your goals if they are indeed in line with your goals. Using our earlier example, suppose your company's new division becomes a major success under your able guise and direction. Will your success help you to achieve what you consider essential in your life (a larger salary, more visibility, etc.)? If so, you can look forward to meeting these objectives by taking action. If not, your success will have minimal impact, and thus shouldn't be a concern.

Either way, this exercise will reveal that your presumed success shouldn't cause you to be fearful at all.

Dealing with the fear that causes you to procrastinate is the most effective way to disarm it. As with facing the fear of failure, you'll find that your fear of success is mostly unfounded.

How to Overcome Perfectionism

First what you have to do is create a line between achieving a perfect result and a near-perfect result as well as the rewards that come with both results. You would eventually realize that the difference is negligible, almost unnoticeable and absolutely not worth the stress.

Second, consider the costs of being a perfectionist. Think of the many ways in which perfectionism is a liability. One it leads to great stress and fatigue as well as paralyzing you into a state of inaction.

Third, question why you want to be perfect. In most cases, you'll find there's no justifiable reason. Instead, there's an intrinsic fear of being unable to meet expectations, even when those expectations are unrealistic.

Lastly, realize that your efforts can deliver value even if your work is imperfect. For example, scoring 95% on an exam may be less appealing than receiving a perfect score, but it's better than scoring a 70% or 80%. Mowing your lawn once a week has to value even if your hedges aren't perfectly trimmed. An evening out with your spouse doesn't have to go perfectly for the two of you to fully enjoy each other's company.

All of the above examples point at one thing – perfection is almost needless and often time, not worthwhile. Your inner perfectionist is a tyrant that adds little value to your life. Or as the acclaimed novelist Anne Lamott once said, "Perfectionism is the voice of the oppressor." Quiet that voice, and you'll be less inclined to procrastinate.

How to Overcome Fear of Failure

First, realize that fear of failure is part of human nature. Our egos are entwined with our ability to succeed in whatever we pursue. The idea that we might fail is vexing to us.

Second, redefine the meaning of failure as it relates to your life. Rather than defining it as the result of a character flaw – e.g., you're destined to fail because you're imperfect – redefine it as simple feedback that a given action or tactic isn't working. Once you do so, you can come up with a different approach that has a greater chance of success. In other words, view failure as useful data rather than an indignity you're forced to endure.

Third, consider that some of the world's most successful people failed miserably at various points in their lives. Their failures didn't stop them from achieving greatness. On the contrary, failure propelled them forward, filling them with the desire to succeed.

A very good example is the case of Abraham Lincoln losing so many elections before finally winning the presidential election. Another inspiring example is the case of filmmaker Steven Spielberg who was rejected by the University of Southern California three times due to poor grades. JK Rowling, the author of the highly successful Harry Porter series, claims she "failed on an epic scale" but her failure drove her to success. The first example went on to become one of the most revered and respected world leaders, while the latter two are billionaires and respected figures in film and literature respectively.

To overcome the fear of failure, think about the worst possible outcome. It's probably not as bad as you imagine. Then, redefine what failure means to you. Consider how you might leverage it – remember, it's just feedback – rather than letting it stop you from taking action.

Chapter 5: Seeking Mentors

The pace of life is undoubtedly increasingly faster. All aspects of our life undergone major changes. There are frequent and complex social changes happening, and there are constant growth and evermore new inventions and improvements. Due to these numerous and constant changes, individuals have to deal with a great deal of pressure. If care is not taken, we can end up being isolated from the rest of the world as a result of these needs and circumstances.

We cannot equip ourselves single-handedly to cope with all these changes and challenges. Any person hell-bent on conquering the world by themselves without seeking the help or guidance of anyone will resign to a life of frustration, hardship, stress, sadness, possible mediocrity, and eventual failure.

No matter who we are at a stage of our life, no matter the level of our experience, we need the guidance, support, and advice of others to shape, confirm or direct our personal and professional life. Simply put, we all need Mentors.

A mentor is someone who can guide us, help us, nurture and enhance our personal or professional quest for growth and development. The traditional method of seeking mentorship was by seeking out an older person in that field or someone with more experience and success in that field. Nowadays, the emphasis is put more on the knowledge, information, network, and influence of the mentor.

Mentoring can be sought in two distinct areas of our life:

- Personal Growth
- Professional Growth

We seek an informal mentor to contribute to making us a better person and be comfortable with ourselves, which eventually leads to us becoming a better citizen of the world.

Personal Growth is all about honing on life skills such as relationships with family, interpersonal skills with colleagues and acquaintances, getting on with others, accepting oneself, confidence, self-esteem, and integrity.

Generally, we may seek a mentor for personal, social and spiritual growth. Such a person can be anyone that we regard to be experienced, respectable and wise.

When it comes to professional growth, we seek mentors to enhance professional growth and move up the career ladder faster.

Professional Growth is all about gaining and developing the required skills and competencies needed to stay relevant and equipped in our jobs and professions.

Benefits of Seeking Mentors:
1. Mentoring can be gained from an experienced person, someone with a particular skill, outlook, perspective or experience. Seeking advice based on specific skills or expertise, seeking help and support in areas that we need to grow and develop
2. It helps us get the needed insight from someone who has gone through what we are yet to, and someone who has achieved what we set out to.
3. Our mentor can help us to carry out an honest and comprehensive personal analysis in order to determine our strength and weakness. Our mentor then helps us capitalize and make effective use of those strengths, as well as overcoming those weaknesses.

4. Having a mentor comes with feedback, approval, and confirmation with regards to our actions and decisions.

5. Seeking mentors is a long-term commitment and profound investment in our future.

6. A Mentor helps us with our goal-setting, challenges us to grow beyond our perceived or self-imposed limitations. A mentor helps us to keep us in line, ensuring that we stay on the right track to achieve our goals.

7. Mentors are likely to introduce us to crucial and influential individuals that are the greats and the goods in our professional life. These individuals are exactly who we need to achieve our set-out goals and objectives.

Chapter 6: Misconceptions and Mistakes to Avoid

At the beginning of practicing mindful meditation, you are most likely going to feel discomfort, and you might become restless very quickly.

This is because the brain is a stranger to having such a low level of stimulus, which it tries to counter by sending signals to the body to make it restless. Think of this as your body protesting to your actions.

When these feelings kick in, stay in it is your responsibility to stay right on track and not give. Exercise control over your mind.

Many people have some misconceptions regarding meditation. Those misconceptions make it even more difficult for them to commit to the moment, focus and continue their mindfulness practice. The most common of these misconceptions is that meditation is designed to clear your mind of all thoughts, which means when a thought pops in your mind, you become annoyed and frustrated thinking you are not doing the meditation the right way.

Well, this is completely wrong. In fact, being distracted during meditation by your thoughts is not such a bad thing; it becomes an avenue for you to exercise control. Every time you are distracted by a thought, you gain further control over your mind when you are able to go back to being the focus.

Another misconception common among beginners is to think any feeling of awkwardness at the start of meditational practice is wrong. This is very wrong. In fact, it is expected of you to experience these things at the beginning – it is a sign of being a newbie.

So, commit to your mindful practices, do not quite easily, and give it time and most especially, give yourself the needed time to acclimatize to new conditions.

Public Speaking

The act of public speaking constitutes a huge challenge for many. The fear continues for a long time and for many, it affects them constantly. The notion of public speaking is not limited to just giving speeches – you have carried out public speaking the moment you have talked to someone you are not familiar with.

The average person fears public speaking because they lack self-confidence. These people do not believe in themselves and fear they will be judged by their peers and appear uneducated. This is an unnecessary fear—public speaking is one of the easiest things to do and can be mastered by just following a few simple steps.

The first step to overcoming this challenge is to determine and assess your audience through some social determinants like age group, social status, social class, level of education etc. When an audience is targeted, this gives the ability to build some credibility - which the audience would definitely reciprocate, showing you the respect and attention you warrant.

This is crucial - if credibility is lost, you are doomed to fail. Imagine for a second that you are talking to an acquaintance at work that you are not very familiar with. You would not want to bring up a controversial topic such as a political issue or a stance on religious matters—there is a great possibility that you will end up alienating the person if you strike a nerve or two.

Instead, bring up a topic that is generally accepted as small talk; sports, popular and trending TV shows, and movies, or some breaking news that is relevant but not controversial. These things will present you as relevant, in vogue and friendly. Through this idle chat, you can gain information about their stances and personal lives, and make this is a basis for future interactions.

Being liked is always a huge advantage when it comes to how you view yourself. Another easy strategy to improve your public speaking is very simple, but not often utilized—practice.

If you know you are going to see a peer—whether it be a fellow student, a co-worker, or even someone you often see on your commute, rehearsing a few lines of dialogue before you encounter them will leave you ready to say something interesting. It might sound extra but it actually works.

When you have the conversation with the person, you will appear to be quick-thinking and bright, and the other person will likely appreciate you thinking of them. This will result in their opinion of you grow, which makes it easier to approach them in the future. The best way to practice a conversation or speech is in a mirror, alone. If you can speak to yourself, you can speak to others as well. This seems too obvious, but it is more beneficial than one might think.

The final step in overcoming the fear of public speaking is to have a healthy image of yourself. What you think of yourself is what others can relate to, talk to or like.

Chapter 7: Focus On Managing Your Energy Not Your Time

Manage Your Energy

To efficiently manage your time, you need to start with energy management techniques. Numerous time management guides treat "Time" as an infinitely manageable resource. As if by simply planning your day more meticulously, you will be able to make the most of your allocated hours and get more done than ever before. However, the truth is managing time isn't that simple. There are so many complexities to the management of time that makes it near-impossible.

It is impossible to have a productive day at work when you don't have enough energy for it. As much as planning and scheduling are important, management is just as important, or even more so.

Here is a note on three very essential factors in your life to better understand how your energy levels affect your overall productivity.

Diet for a Productive Day

Each individual is unique, and their dietary approaches are unique too. By eating processed and carb based foods on a regular, you are depriving your body of the needed and essential vitamins. A more balanced diet offers more than eating processed foods.

A balanced and healthy diet enhances your brainpower and keeps you focused and productive throughout the day. Your body breaks the food you consume to mostly glucose. Glucose act as your body's fuel that runs your body and brain.

Carbs release glucose gradually in the blood and keep your body active throughout the day, giving you the energy you need to work throughout the day. Eat a whole grain food based diet. Here are a few tips for managing your energy level.

- Never skip breakfast: Breakfast being the most important meal of the day is not a myth, it is factual and scientifically proven. Don't skip breakfast any day, ensure that you eat a healthy breakfast every morning. A healthy breakfast will help you stay active all day. Include complex carbs such as whole grain bread and cereals as part of your breakfast regimen.

- Eat small, but frequent and regular meals: Eat small, but frequent meals throughout the day. This style of eating will keep your blood pressure stable and provide enough energy to stay active all day. The point here is to feel satisfied and nourished, not overfed and stuffed.

- Eat foods that are rich in fiber and drink enough water: always eat food that is rich in fiber and drink at least 8 glasses of water daily. This combination is not just essential for healthy living, it is also easy to do.

- Caffeine and alcohol: Only drink a moderate amount of coffee during the day. Use a teacup to drink coffee. Most people wrongly think a large amount of coffee would keep you active throughout the day, but drinking excessive coffee may result in a productivity-impairing crash. When you drink alcohol or any alcoholic drink after having your dinner, it interferes with your sleep. This is not ideal and it is advisable that you avoid drinks like that before bedtime.

Must-Eat Foods for a Productive Day

The following are must-eat foods that should form be ever-present in your daily meal.

- Salmon: Salmon, especially wild variety is rich in omega-3, Vitamin-B, and iron. Salmon helps to improve brain activity and keep your mind focused.
- Berries: Berries are rich in antioxidants, and this allows them to boost your memory, increase the efficiency of the mind as well as body coordination.
- Eggs: Organic eggs are rich in Vitamin-B, and the vitamin is responsible for improving memory.
- Eggplant: Eggplants helps to improve the communication signals between messenger molecules and brain cells.
- Green Tea: Green tea contains useful antioxidants, as well as a neuroprotective effect that helps the nervous system work faster and efficiently.
- Dark leafy greens: by eating dark leafy greens, you are ensuring a productive day. The irons, minerals, and phytonutrients in the food help in supplying more oxygen to the brain cells and improving cognitive control.
- Dark and milk chocolate: Dark chocolate puts focus and concentration at the optimum while milk chocolate improves visual and verbal memory as well as speeding up reaction time.
- Calcium-rich foods: Calcium, taken through your diet keeps the nervous system in perfect working condition. Foods such as milk, cheese, green vegetables, and beans provide quality calcium.
- Yogurt: Low-fat yogurt contains probiotics, proteins, and minerals. Yogurt helps your digestive system, and

studies show that probiotics in the yogurt help in increasing the life span of the body cells, eventually resulting in a longer life.

Foods that Lower Your Productivity

The above are food options that contribute to increased productivity, the following foods offer the reverse.

- Sugar-rich foods and drinks make you confused, nervous, anxious and oftentimes weak.
- Food with high-calorie content such as hamburger and fries will slow you down and make you sleepy at work. When you combine this with the large cup of coffee you took in the morning, the result is even worse.
- Eating inadequately is not helpful for your productivity. This will make you slow to react and develop an inability to remember things.

Exercise and Have a Productive Life

Exercise improves your physical health, and it also increases your productivity at work. The benefits of exercise:

- Exercise provides your body energy and makes you alert: Exercise boost blood flow to the brain and help you stay sharp to tackle challenging work situations. Exercise gives you the required energy to complete a task or activity.
- Improves overall workability: Daily exercise improves your health and gives you more stamina to manage the physical demands of work. A fit and strong body will make you less prone to workplace injury.
- Exercise leads to a feeling of accomplishment, happiness, and joy.
- Improves mental health: Studies show that exercise improves mental health, lower anxiety, and depression. Exercise increases the production of a "feel-good" hormone known as serotonin. Serotonin helps to improve your mood and promotes a general feeling of wellness and comfort. You have noticed that when you are stress-free and in a good mood, you finish complex tasks quickly.
- Helps avoid sickness: with the help of regular exercise, your immune system is more effective in avoiding sickness, illness and health conditions such as obesity, diabetes and other heart-related diseases such as hypertension and high blood pressure.

Make exercise a part of your life

- Walk faster when mowing the lawn
- Don't drive, walk your kids to school and jog home
- Swim, whenever there is a chance
- Instead of driving to the nearby cinema, grocery store or department store, you can walk.
- Mix some light exercise with your TV time (and also Netflix and chill time)
- Finish your housework quickly
- Walk the dog regularly
- Walk faster when going to the bus stop or train station
- Do some light exercise during your lunchtime
- Exercise with your neighbor – this not only helps you but also creates a friendly atmosphere with your neighbor.

Do things that you like

- Pick up an activity and make it habitual: examples include dancing, bicycling, horseback riding
- Play a sport: tennis, baseball, basketball, soccer or football.

Small changes will make you productive with a few days.

Your Sleep Schedule

You cannot downplay the role of quality sleep in your ability to wake up as early as possible, and still feel refreshed, renewed, energized and eager to start your day.

Your body produces some hormones such as dopamine and adrenaline which keep your focus, alert and inspired on the job. Irregular sleep time, as well as a short period of sleep, lower the production of these hormones, hence leading to a reduction in productivity.

A few studies have shown that a sufficient amount of sleep at night helps people to remember and process new information better, make them more resilient and creative at work. With quality sleep, you are able to process better and recollect old information leading to a sharper mind – and eventually leading to increased productivity.

For people engaged in tasking challenges such as examinations and stressful workload, quality sleep would do more good than harm. It would help get your focus levels at their optimum and performance level at maximum.

Tips for better quality sleep

- Maintain a fixed bedtime: Fix a bedtime and keep to it, regardless of your schedule or even if it is the weekend. If you make an adjustment with your bedtime, compensate by taking a short nap during the day.

- Wake-up at the same time daily: train your body to wake up at the same time daily. Say you take about 7-8 hours to sleep daily, you would wake up around the same time if you keep to your schedule. You wouldn't even have a need for an alarm.
- Don't sleep before your bedtime: Some days you may feel sleepy after dinner. Avoid going to bed and do a mildly stimulating activity such as walking or washing the dishes and avoid sleeping. The point is to stay on schedule as to not disrupt your body makeup.
- Turn off your Computer and TV before bed: Don't engage in stimulating games or watch violent TV shows before going to sleep. These stimulating activities delay the sleeping process. This leads to a disruption in the sleep schedule.
- Make use of an e-reader when reading and stay away from devices with backlighting such as iPad for reading.
- Keep your bedroom dark and cool, the ideal temperature should be about 18C.
- Sleep on a comfortable bed or mattress – it is not just healthy, it is simply comfy.

Things you should avoid before sleep

- Avoid having a heavy dinner just before bedtime. This will inhibit digestion and make you feel sick afterward. Keep your supper/dinner light and don't go to sleep immediately after eating.

- Avoid drinking alcohol or any form of alcoholic drink before sleep. Alcohol before bedtime leads to shallow sleep.
- Avoid taking caffeine or substances with caffeine like coffee
- Also, don't smoke before bedtime
- Don't take sleeping pills, unless recommended by a medical practitioner.

Conclusion

The process of change from impulsive procrastinator to goal accomplisher means making an internal change that includes learning and growth. This helps transform who we are, how we see ourselves, how we are viewed by others, what we think of other people, and how we interact with the world around us.

If you still aren't sure where to start, then begin with these small tips to jump start you:

Pick at least 5 things you can get done tomorrow. If you really were committed to making a change and proving to yourself that you are capable, you can power through almost anything. Begin with 5 things, even those that have nothing to do with your ending goal, and do them within 24 hours. Put yourself on a clock and make sure you complete them before the deadline. When you repeat this over a period of time, you become used to it and eventual a part and parcel of you.

Start with positive thinking and mindfulness to stay in the present moment. Stay away from negative energy of whatever form – there is nothing as harmful as self-sabotage. The journey of harnessing your mind is a continuous one and it never hurts to strive for the peak of your potentials.

By having better control of your emotions and overall balance over yourself, you become a better person.

One of the most important things to truly change your habits from laziness to discipline is to approach the change from the viewpoint of positive addition instead of punitive subtraction. This means to think about one thing you will add to your day, instead of something you are giving up or letting go. When you use the viewpoint of positive addition, the change becomes easier. An example is the case of people who change their diet with the addition of vitamins, leafy greens, and green tea.

They see the addition of more control, or the ability to feel better after eating.

To approach change from a positive, addition standpoint makes you automatically begin to feel as if you are receiving instead of losing. On the other hand, those who approach change by thinking of what they must give up, like time or "favorite foods," feel deprived. For a healthy and lasting change, deprivation is never a good option. It creates a sense of animosity in the person, with various parts of your body rebelling to the changes.

Or you'll feel physically better from sticking to a healthy routine. Begin to see yourself in this new life by visualizing yourself as a disciplined person and begin acting today as if this is true. It is also easier to stay committed to a healthy addition than to stay committed to the removal of unhealthy favorites.

It's never too late to start this process. There is award or recognition for starting a change earlier, this is a personal unique phenomenon that is specific to each person, so time and "being too late" are all irrelevant. Where will you be in 5 years? Those 5 years are going to pass, how will you wish you spent that time? Nobody is keeping score or watching to ensure that you have perfection. Most people are busy living their own lives and don't have the time to monitor the happening in other people's life. This is real-life and you are what that matters.

Other than our supportive cheerleaders, nobody is out there watching to see if we succeed or fail. They don't expect us to make it by a certain time, and there is no scorekeeper waiting to see if we are able to complete the race in record time.

Therefore, start making those changes today, but go at a pace that you can continue without burning out and sabotaging yourself – which is the most important thing.

No matter what, your life will improve the second you commit to having a better-disciplined life! That right there is a fact.

www.ingramcontent.com/pod-product-compliance
Lightning Source LLC
Chambersburg PA
CBHW040230240726
48664CB00001B/80